wanders of the night

Keilah Belen

Keilah Belen

Copyright © 2017 Keilah Belen

All rights reserved.

ISBN: 1981960864
ISBN-13: 978-1981960866

To the sweetest and strongest woman I know,
my Grandma.
And the person who inspired me to stick to my passion.
Thank you for sharing your greatest passion with me
and believing in me. I used to throw away my pieces.
Now here I am.

Thank you for everything.

CONTENTS

Acknowledgements: i
An Angel: 1
I Don't Sleep with Pillows: 3
Unspoken Time: 4
A Sign: 5
Letter to the Under-appreciated: 6
Seasons in Me: 7
Something There: 8
Lost: 10
She is Power: 11
Contemplation of Self: 12
A Risk: 13
The Battle: Inside vs. Outside: 14
Just Don't: 15
On My Knees: 17
For Once: 18
Something More: 19
We Were Nine: 20
When: 21
It's You: 22
Inconsistency: 23
Independence: 24
The Stories Untold: 25
The Water Cycle: 26
Different Paths: 27
I Can't Say Never Now: 28
Music to My Ears: 29
The Hurting: 30
March 16: 31
Truthfully: 32
The Ones Who Love Wholeheartedly: 33
Meant for More: 34

Let it Be: 35
Two Lost Souls: 36
Trust the Process: 37
The Giving Tree: 38
Beneath the Surface: 39
The Romantic Science of Covalent Bonding: 40
Perfectly Aligned: 41
Death Petals: 42
Here We Go Again: 43
The Perfect Song: 44
Broken Hearts: 45
A Hidden Treasure: 46
The Battle: Inside vs. Outside II: 47
Erupting Heart: 48
Time in Healing: 50
Starving for Sanity: 51
Awaiting Destination: 52
Cliff Hanger: 53
The Soul in Soldier: 54
Deep Waters: 55
My Artistry: 56
The Roots and Her Growth: 57
Dig Deeper: 58
Rise Above the Surface: 59
Home in Your Arms: 60
Exhaling the Toxic: 61
Home is Where the Heart Is: 62
The Broken Will Rise: 63
Her Discoveries in Hurting: 64
The Night Sky in Me: 65
Behind the Empty Hearted: 66
Love Injection: 67
A Part of You Everywhere: 68
Dear Dad: 69

Silencing the Heart:: 71
All on Me: 72
Hurting for the Hurt: 73
If I Never Get the Chance: 74
Begging for Mercy: 76
Notetaking I: 77
Killer Brain: 79
Realization: 80
Lightning Bolt: 81
Dear Grandma: 82
A Dying Rose: 83
Ghost Poet: 84
Viewpoint: 85
Lonely Hours: 86
Toxic Ozone: 87
Unfadeable Memories: 88
The Battle: Inside vs. Outside III: 89
My Potent Poesy: 90
Tell Me Now: 91
Chin Up: 92
Who?: 93
Unfazed Heartbreak: 94
Euphoric Facade: 95
The Battle: Inside vs. Outside IV: 96
Notetaking II: 97
Homeless: 98
Climate Change: 99
What We Fear: 100
Reminder: 101
Wish You Were Here: 102
The Night in Day: 103
Heartbreak: 104
Moving On From Loss and Heartbreak I: 105
Moving On From Loss and Heartbreak II: 106

Moving On From Loss and Heartbreak III: 107
Distant: 108
Open Wounds: 109
Notetaking III: 110
Phenomenal: 111
The Unexpected: 112
Fighter: 113
All Over Again: 114
Your Graveyard: 115
November: 116
His Showing: 117
The Battle: Inside vs. Outside V: 119

This book contains my deepest thoughts, from dawn to dusk. There are still many that are unspoken and unwritten, but here's a start. I am forever grateful for the memories created-- good and bad. I am appreciative of everything that has broken me; they have shaped me into the person I am now.

These pieces are unorganized: shifting from either feeling lost and crushed to the core to finding it in me to stay faithful and stable. Altogether, it is a book consisting of the battles in my mind. The words I cannot speak of are expressed on these pages, and there is a bit of everything in hopes to bring warmth to those of you who constantly struggle to find peace.

Enjoy.

An Angel

In this world, there are people who know of Him,
And there are people who don't.
Those knowledgeable
Know the evil and the miracles capable of occurring with His love.
People like me know there's a heaven;
There is hell.
And there are demons, too.
Evil spirits;
Society is one.
It tries to swallow you into different beliefs.
Mine are of His.
But along the way, there are angels, too.
There are angels that are sent by Him,
Who guide, shield, and look after you.
I've had many guide me through what seems to be the right path.
But angels come in human forms, too.

When I feel lonely,
the thought of you accompanies me.
When I'm fearful,
The thought of you protects me.
When I can't seem to get through a long, dreadful day,
The thought of you helps me battle my conflict.
These are all verbifications that describe an angel.

You're a beautiful soul.
You're lost.
But that's okay.

Keilah Belen

You've touched people's hearts,
But you've done more to mine than anybody else's.
You've made me want to become closer to Him.
In my everyday thoughts,
Many things remind me of you.
You're a cloud.
Clouds come in many forms, too.

A polar stratospheric cloud;
Glowing brightly with vivid iridescent colors.
For the way you make me feel inside.
A cirrostratus cloud;
Capable of forming halos around the sun like a white veil.
This is how angelic you are.
(I've witnessed and captured pictures of these before and it's astonishing.)
A cumulus cloud;
Puffy, cotton-like and give such calming shade.
This is how safe you make me feel.
A nimbostratus cloud;
Dark, widespread, and a formless layer.
For the times you feel lost and absent, drowning in your thoughts.
A cumulonimbus cloud;
Shaped densely and associated with thunderstorms.
For an electrifying soul you attain.

I fear storms,
But not you.
You're such angelic nature,
Created and sent by Him.
What a true rarity.
Angels come in human forms, too.

I Don't Sleep with Pillows

Endless pillow thoughts,
Make me wonder.
What am I most afraid of?
It's ending my life,
Not being closer to Him.
Not knowing my fullest potential of His faith

Endless pillow thoughts,
Make me wonder…
I've never been a colorful flower,
One to blossom,
Allowing the world to see my true colors.
But you've seen these petals blossom.
As time goes by,
More and more seem to reveal themselves.

Endless pillow thoughts,
Make me wonder…

With you,
Like the nature of a flower,
It's an instinct.

Endless pillow thoughts,
Make me wonder…
Don't blossom.
Your petals will fall off quicker.
Don't do it.
Slow down.
Stop.

Endless pillow thoughts,
Make me wonder…
I'm afraid of losing you, too.

Unspoken Time

Days, weeks, months, and years--
They have all passed
With rolling tears and agonizing pain.
An ordinary routine.

Days, weeks, months, and years--
They have all passed
With graciousness, laughs, and smiles.
An ordinary routine.

Days, weeks, months, and years--
They have all passed
With unspoken words no one knows of.

A Sign

God show me a sign.
Is this really meant to be?

You know my pains.
You know my life.
You know all of me.

The way I feel,
I can't help it.
If this isn't meant to be,
Then why do this to me?

Shall I help him heal?
Shall I help him feel?

God show me a sign,
If this is really meant to be.

Keilah Belen

Letter to the Under-appreciated

I'm proud of you. I'm proud of how you keep yourself together, even though you're falling apart on the inside. I'm proud of how genuine and kind you remain, how you still treat others with respect. I'm proud of how considerate you are of others' feelings, because I know how it feels to be on the other end of the stick. I'm proud of how far you've come, and I know it has not been easy to remain patient with others who don't think twice about their actions or words. I know it's not easy to remain patient with your own battles, but I'm proud that you keep pushing through this dark world. You may feel dim to others, but you're a freaking lightning bolt to me. This world needs more phenomena like you, so from the bottom of my heart Thank You.

Seasons in Me

Sometimes I give off Summer

Sometimes Winter

Constantly intertwined

Falling in between

Giving too much warmth

Or too many cold nights

One thing is for sure

I Spring way too fast

Into my thoughts

The constant battle

Of giving too much

Or giving too little

The effects

Of a used up heart

Keilah Belen

<u>Something There</u>

I can't feel, but I do.
I can't explain, but I do.
I can't. I can't. I can't.
With you I do.

I'm numb,
I'm vacant.
Sometimes I feel everything.
Sometimes I feel nothing.

I feel things with you.
I feel nothing with everybody else.
I can't seem to understand.

What is this?
Is this spiritual?
Is this real?

I lay in bed.
Constantly contemplating.
Constant can'ts and constant cans.

Never been enough for someone else.
Never allowed it either way.
Show me that there's something there.

I don't Expose Enormous Emotions.
I got Recurring Raging Rainy days.
I'm Scouring, Scraping Senseless shit.
I can't Filter Fucking Feelings.

This isn't loneliness like the days before you came through.
I'm just as confused as you.
So why do I feel the way I do?
I can't feel, but I do with you.

Keilah Belen

Lost

A lot of times people find their way back to You.
A lot of times it's because they've been lost.
They've been stripped of all emotions
With nothing to do and nowhere to go.

Time gets lost.
So does their Soul.
The deeper you dig in, the emptier the hole.
A vacant chest and empty heart.

I'm trying to piece together
Why that time hasn't come for me yet.
Dark times have passed for my brothers.
Their Souls and Spirits are set.
I guess mine is stuck in between--
In between two fucking rocks where I can't be seen.
Nowhere to reach.
So just give me my last sign and preach to me.

Dig in deeper to my soul.
Take whatever pain I have as a whole.
Rip me apart into all that's left,
and turn it into something more.
Turn this into Yours.

Take me up to heaven,
Do I have to suffer more?
In order to realize my Soul should be all Yours

She is Power

She doesn't live up to anyone's expectations.
She makes her own.
She is a soft kind of powerful.

She's closed up like a book you'll never read.
She has never needed anyone to pick her up.
She stands independently, unfit for this world.

She drags herself down.
She rarely knows how great she is.

And you'll never be able to reach her untouched Soul
Without an effort to search what hurts her in the first place.

Keilah Belen

Contemplation of Self

Maybe I think too much.
I don't say a lot.

Maybe I say I'm too much.
Or I'm just not enough.

A Risk

No. I don't know all of you,
But I know enough.
No. I don't agree with some of your decisions,
But I don't care.
No. I have never accepted these actions before,
But I will.
No. I have never had true love,
But I'll risk my heart for you.

Yes. I'm lost,
But you're piecing me back together.
Yes. I'm falling,
But are you?

I'll take all of you,
If you take all me.

The Battle: Inside vs. Outside

My flesh is furious.
It is flaming and scorching.
It is smoking and sizzling.
It is burning, and it is blazing.

My protection. My shield. My armor.
A fire extinguisher.
The thin layer of tissue covering my body,
Covering all of its sufferings.
The sheath.

My skin.

Just Don't

Please don't get close to me.
Don't suck the living the soul,
The smallest bit remaining out of me.
Don't stretch me apart.

Because once you get inside me,
I mean the real me, all of me:
My past, my darkest secrets,
The obstacles I've had to overcome,
And the shit people have put me through—

Once you get to know my fear of the undiscovered seas
And the unknown creatures that lie in the ocean so deep—
How nauseous the universe and galaxies make me feel—
And how the sound of a terrible thunderstorm makes me
tremble—

When you get to know every aspect of me
And the details that shape who I am,
And why I have these continuous thoughts in my head
That make me lose hours of sleep—

Once you get inside of me,
You will wonder how a person like me
Could go through all these things
And act like everything is fine.

There are only 2 things that will happen:
You will either grow too close and capture feelings,
But end up leaving
Because you could not grasp the idea of committing
And later realize what an asshole you are
For being another bullet point to the list of things that have

hurt me.
Like another bullet to the chest.
When you realize this,
You will come back,
But it will be too late.
The only other thing that can happen,
Is to stay.
You will fall for me.

I am a heartbreaker.
The only way for that to happen,
Is to get inside of me.
The only way for that to happen,
Is if you fuck up.
Your heart will internally bleed and splatter
From self-loathing after ruining something so pure.
You just ripped yourself apart
Because you couldn't keep me.

Because if you lose me,
It wasn't me.
It was you.

So if you're going to get close to me,
Bring in your best battle.
Otherwise, Don't.

On My Knees

Lord, tonight I spoke to you.
I was feeling all sorts of blue.
On the floor, I'm lost and insecure.
I can't take this anymore.

Crying and begging,
Shaking and shivering.
Begging for more energy.
Begging for patience and strength.

Heaven and earth—
I'm trying to reach you,
But we're on different wavelengths.
But I need you more than ever.
I want to serve you forever.

Too long I've been carefree,
But I'm ready.

Show me your love.

Keilah Belen

<u>For Once</u>

I'm in too deep.
I need to know
If you feel the same for me.

I need to know.
Should I stay,
Or should I go?

Just a random flower, far from a rose.
I'm nowhere near perfection.
Can't help this temptation.

Just look.
Look inside.
Look deeper.
Look at me.

Something More

Mental connections
Over physical attractions
Baby with you it's both temptations

Because when I look at you,
It's Eye to Eye.
Heart to Heart.
Mind to Mind.

And I'm not going to lie.
I'll put my heart on the line.
I'm not wasting any time.

When it comes to you,
All I do is speak the truth.
I promise nothing feels as good
As a night when I talk to you.
Just imagine when it all comes true.

All I want to say
Is that I'll never walk away.
All you have to do is tell me that you'll stay.

And every night I lay awake--
Thinking maybe you're my next mistake,
Thinking maybe you're my next heartache.

I don't care about the cards you've been dealt.
If I told you how I really felt--
Look into my eyes and say my name,
Would you say the same?

Keilah Belen

We Were Nine

Call it luck.
Call it whatever you want.
Deep inside our hearts we feel left out.
We were nine,
So Together we can justify
That what we saw is forever instilled in our minds.
We are not free.
We cannot stop what we see.
We pay the price emotionally.
We saw it all.
We feel it all.
At the end of the day,
God saved us all.

When?

After what we came to be,
The only presence I've encountered--
The only touch I've ever felt of you--
The only time I've looked into your eyes--
The only time I've ever felt security--
Is in my dreams. Right next to you.

It seems like next time will never come.
There is nothing more that I crave than to be with you.

It's You

You don't get to tell me I deserve better.
Because I want you. I chose you.
You are what makes my sun shine brighter.
You are my sanity in this crazy world.
You lift me higher.
I choose you.
So please choose me, too.

Inconsistency

I need to see that you care.

I need for you to show me.

I need more than what you display

Or words you sometimes say.

Effort please.

Keilah Belen

<u>Independence</u>

There's a difference.
I am alone not lonely.

I was put into this world
To succeed by myself
Without a man.

I was put into this world
To establish my own empire
Without a man.

Because I am Strong
Capable of doing anything I aspire.

The Stories Untold

Always be kind to others.

Always be aware of other's emotions.

Always offer your hand to those in need,

For you do not know of the stories untold.

Keilah Belen

<u>The Water Cycle</u>

No hope when I look at the sky. It's covered in nimbostratus, cumulonimbus clouds. And so the day is dark—no light, nothing to have faith in.

These clouds are heavy, filled with all emotions a human can possibly contain—good and bad. All the hope, faith, love. All the pain. I'm almost convinced these clouds are the shadowing bad spirits that act like aid.

Every day is a living storm. Every day is rainy. The clouds release these drops of rain—maybe drops of hope to give me. Drip. Drip. Drip. Onto my tearing skin. A chance to heal. Strip. Strip. Strip. By the time I have a chance to absorb and recover, they hit the ground, with a bit more of me. My spirit bonds with these droplets, melts into the ground, ready to evaporate. No hope. No mending.

Different Paths

We used to talk late at night,
Talking of the things that set us aside.
I guess the chances that I thought we had was slight.

And now I lay awake, hands tied
Hands untied on a keyboard where I just write.
Maybe things would change if I just tried.
For days I think and think and no words typed,
Staring into blank pages like blank space; it's all white.

I wished and wished,
Hoping that tomorrow would be the first night
That I could finally see you at midnight.
I'm sure you'd be the spotlight, the highlight,
Just downright the sunlight
That ignites my insides,
Something so bright that I can't hide.

Where we both see eye to eye
A path where we both unite
And walk together side by side
But I know something isn't right
This is where we divide
Because it's a one-way sight

Keilah Belen

I Can't Say Never Now

I had never seen such charm in a man.
I had never seen such grace.
I had never been able to admire such artistry--
Until I met you.

There is charm in your eyes.
There is charm in your smile.
There is charm in the way you laugh.
There is charm in the words you speak.

There is grace in the sparkle of your eyes.
There is grace in your bright smile.
There is grace in your dorky laugh.
There is grace in the truth behind the words you speak.

When you play your instrument,
It's more than just music playing.
The rhythm and beats are the deep places
In your heart you do not speak of.
I had never been able to admire such artistry.

Until I met you.

Music to My Ears

He welcomed me with wide open arms,

But that's not how I knew he was the one

Who would forever hold my heart.

It was the way his heart beat—

A thorough rhythm,

Beautifully pouncing out of his chest

So soundly,

Parallel to mine.

Keilah Belen

<u>The Hurting</u>

You know the feeling you get
When your heart is hurting
So badly you take your hand
And place it on your chest
A knot in your throat
Tears streaming down
An overflowed river
After a severe storm
That's what this is.

March 16

It was a great day.
The sun-- Not too hot.
The clouds-- Not too cloudy.
The wind-- Not too windy.

It was a great day.
We could feel the positive vibes
That were shared between us all
For just one great day.

But all that changed
In just a blink of an eye.
Like in the books and movies
Literally.

If there could be a day
I could erase from my past
It would be this day
The day that haunts me… Us.

I've seen terrible things before
And I've experienced the worst of life
But this day is another picture
Added to my scrapbook of bad memories

You see pain in characters
In films that make you tear up
But none of that compares
To this pain

The pain I saw in their eyes
The fear of not making it through
The discomfort of their injuries
Is all the pain my heart feels.

Keilah Belen

Truthfully

After everything that has happened
I've learned to appreciate the smallest of things
And even the people who I hold dear to my heart

After everything that has happened
You can't expect me to keep my feelings silent
Because in a blink of an eye
What if I was gone?

What if the words I told you in the past,
Were the last words
You could ever cling on to.

You have to understand
That my perspective of life
And my perspective of you
Has changed

After everything that has happened
I expected some understanding from you
As to how I feel and how I act
As to why I want you all to myself

But I must apologize now
Because you can't understand
And that's because maybe I cared too much
From the beginning

And now I'm trapped
Feeling this way for you

And this time…
I destroyed what could've been
Unintentionally

The Ones Who Love Wholeheartedly

We love and we care. And we do it wholeheartedly and so thoroughly that we tend to feel responsible for other's sorrow. We generate this feeling of tenderness, making us believe that we're frail because we love so much that the pain other's feel ruptures our heart.

We wish and wish that we could put this load of bricks on our backs so others don't have to walk this road so heavily. But by doing this, we've already managed to carry tons emotionally.

This is when we feel it all. This is when we contemplate our own emotions, our whole purpose of living and breathing.

We can't control our hearts to not feel because they function as our body's circulatory pump. It's a never ending process, just like our lungs naturally cause us to inhale and exhale.

And they do this instinctively, just like we love and care. And no matter what-- whether we force ourselves or hurt to the point of hitting rock bottom-- we won't stop, until our last dying breath.

We just have to accept who we are and that our purpose is to love unconditionally, because at the end of the day we look forward to seeing our loved ones be happy. And that... That's what makes loving and caring worth living for.

Meant for More

You are meant to gather all your tears that stream down your face like a waterfall from misery and pain and create a river, and when you do…

You are meant to make this river function into something much greater, to make it flow into the greatest oceans in this world, and when you do…

You are meant to take the boulders that sit on your back that make you suffer and build sky-high mountains, and when you do…

You are meant to climb these mountains and step on the clouds that lie so effortlessly above them and reach the sky higher than you ever have.

You are meant to take root from the soil that drained you, mend your damaged petals, and sprout larger than expected.

You are meant for the impossible, and you won't stop until you make "the sky is the limit" be limitless.

Let It Be

My brother once told me,
"If it's meant to be, okay.
If it's not meant to be, okay."

And those lines have stuck with me since.
I know for a fact that things happen for a reason.
God puts certain people, obstacles, and events in our life for a reason. And if He wanted that for you, then he would allow it to happen.
So just let it be... Because whatever the outcome may be, you can get through it. You will get through it because that's what's meant to happen.

Keilah Belen

Two Lost Souls

In a world where I don't pay much attention, I paid to you.
I noticed you pondered at random.
I could see it in your eyes—so much grace,
yet so much curiosity.

In a world where I don't pay much attention,
I noticed you'd laugh at the simplest of things.
I could see it in your smile—it's the little things that mattered.

In a world where I don't get too enticed, I was to you.
I noticed your gracious smile and eyes.
But I could see beneath it—fallen between the cracks.
I could read your unreadable pages, written in invisible ink.

In a world where I felt unsure,
I was sure I needed to get to you.

I noticed there was something more.
I could see that I, too, had a similar demeanor.

In a world where I felt incomprehensible, you understood.
You could read me, and I could read you--
Page by page, chapter by chapter.

In a world full of evil, there is God.
And He placed our books in each other's hands.
To seek Him, to find Him, to praise Him.

In a world full of people who step in and out of our lives,
you can't.
You are my best friend, my person, and God's blessing to me.

Trust the Process

You have to let it hurt, then let it go.
Let your sorrow take over and cry it all out.
Cry it all out, so that you are able to collect these tears
And turn them into the greatest oceans.

Once you've done this,
not only have you made bodies of water.
You've drowned your tears and have actually moved them.
So just let it hurt, because in the process you will find that you
are much stronger and capable of defeating
anything this earth
brings you.

Keilah Belen

The Giving Tree

Picture a tree—living for others to admire the beauty of a newly blossomed flower for others to take every so often, living to give off oxygen, living to give others that one moment of peace.

You see, that's all it does. It gives and gives. And in a world like this, it has nothing to take. Nobody pours a drop of water to maintain it.

It waits for an unknowingly pouring day from God, to soak up every inch of rain, every inch of hope to grow and flourish, keeping its trunk high and mighty.

It keeps its branches durable for anything that comes its way. In this process, it keeps producing oxygen, beautiful flowers, and leaves greener than ever that symbolize growth and safety.

It gives; it grows. Without asking for anything in return from this cruel world. That's all it knows. That's its nature. That is me.

<u>Beneath the Surface</u>

To explain what I see in you would be like looking at the night sky and seeing what this universe holds—all the hidden wonders out there are inside your soul waiting to burst out their phenomenal potentials.

It would be like looking at a new moon. You can't see it, but you know it's there. And it makes you wonder—like when I first saw you and knew there was more than just a surface, deep within your core.

It would be like looking at a natural disaster.
Like an earthquake ready to break the surface, generated by the violent shaking of your heart from all its despair.
Like a tornado caused by the never-ending thoughts that rotate rapidly in your head.
Like a natural occurrence of a lightning bolt produced from the electricity that runs in your veins at the touch of a guitar.

It would be like looking into the mountains and the beautiful sceneries of this earth that send out peace and security—just like you make me feel.

Keilah Belen

The Romantic Science of Covalent Bonding

They say that love is a bond-- a bond so strong, a bond that holds people together.

This bond involves the sharing of each other's past stories, darkest secrets, deepest fears, and foggy thoughts. Think of all these as the sharing of electron pairs bounded by two atoms.

This charge of electricity, charge of energy is the stable balance of attractive and repulsive forces. It takes energy to make the bond function; the stronger the love, the stronger the bond.

We can't always see what draws two together; it's unseen. And just like a covalent bond, we are two separate atoms attracted to each other, filling in our orbitals with missing pieces, making our instability stable.

Perfectly Aligned

We laid there, staring at the night sky—something you see in films, something I thought I'd never experience.

Right above us was the bright, shining moon—providing us with perfect lighting to look at each other's faces in such a dark place.

And the glistening stars so perfectly spread out, with clouds surrounding the atmosphere.

And I could feel the connection between us--- filling the vacancy inside me, filling my soul with more than just a touch.

And in that moment, I felt what missing parts we had inside of us and how every moment spent together was literally breathtaking, exchanging the air between us filling in our holes.

I could not understand how someone's presence made me feel so secure; I could not understand how much affection and emotion could run through a person's body.

And I'm looking at him, admiring what a beautiful lost soul he is— and how blessed I was to have crossed paths, scared to never have this moment again.

And the sound of his heart beating next to mine was the perfect duet I would desire listening to on replay for the rest of time.

Keilah Belen

<u>Death Petals</u>

Take my air.
Take it all.

Give me air.
Give me water.
Give me sunlight.
Give me nutrients.

I give.
I give.

wanders of the night

Here We Go Again

We fall in deeper and deeper

Only to separate us

In fear of commitment

In fear of getting hurt

I can feel when you become distant.

The Perfect Song

Do you feel that?

- *Feel what?*

Do you hear that?

- *Hear what?*

Just listen.

(Thump. Thump. Thump.)

- *I feel that. I hear that.*

That, my Love, is the sound of two hearts pounding.
That, my Love, is the sound of a perfect duet I would desire listening to on replay for the rest of time.

Broken Hearts

I can feel it in my chest,
when I take a breath.

I can feel it in my heart,
when I place my fist on it.

I can feel it in my head—
thoughts whisking in my mind,

I can't sleep. I can't eat.

A Hidden Treasure

"You're a gem… so perfect and so pure," he said.
As time passes, I'm coming to realize that in fact I am,
And I am more.

I'm a chest full of brilliance and illumination.
I'm a chest filled with treasure, like never seen before.
I'm a chest, dug deep in the middle of a desert.
I'm a chest… hidden away from everyone,
hidden away from everything.

"I'll never be one to show you off. I don't boast," he said.

But treasure is secluded and concealed for one person's blessed discovery, for that one person who has walked through pouring rain, burning heat, and a stinging snowstorm.

And so God said…

"My child, you have gone through the worst. Here is your aid. This will help you along the way, but child… In that chest you will find valuable pieces, and as soon as you touch it your Soul will know how fortunate it is to have such jewels. You will find that this treasure is stronger than anything you've ever touched, and nothing can destroy it. And the diamonds you hold in your hand will give you confidence, strength, faith, patience, safeness, and love. My child, you must cherish it, and hold it dear to heart. You must remind yourself that I have rewarded you with a gift that cannot be measured. You must admire and appreciate what this chest has brought to your life."

And so He sent you to me, to the eye so beautiful.

The Battle: Inside vs. Outside II

My soul is weary.
It is drowning in this deep ocean inside me.
It is so close to bursting out of my skin.
It is screaming at the top of its lungs,
grasping for air.

But what's to inhale from this toxic world?

My body keeps it in.

"No. You can swim; you can float. You will be the greatest, strongest swimmer any pool, lake, ocean, or body of water has ever come in contact with. So hang in there. You've got this. You've swam for 20 years, and look at the distance you've travelled. No hurricane, no typhoon, no cyclone will sink you down to the bottom in the deepest of waters. Because I am your life jacket, and I will keep you warm through the driest of ice. Keep swimming. I got you."

Keilah Belen

Erupting Heart

My heart is a volcano.
It's so massive,
composed of built up
deteriorating distress,
drenched in hot lava.

That's how it feels like
when it's burning my chest,
because it's so searing
that it's seeping
through the small spaces
of my sensitive skin.

All these years
it has been dormant,
but it's prepared to detonate,
to deluge all of its
despair into my veins.

I can't pick up a pen and write
because if I did—
I'd burn right through the pages
with the ink of my own broiling flesh blood.

Instead, I just keep it all inside
'til my heart turns into natural volcanic glass.
Obsidian.
Because it cools rapidly
after I gather myself for the 100th time,
But it doesn't last for long.

Because it shatters
into a million pieces by nighttime—
slitting the surface of my sacred skin,
while I'm trying to contain these tears
made up of acid rain
that are streaming down,
blistering my face
by the outcome of this
volcanic heart eruption.

Keilah Belen

<u>Time in Healing</u>

Healing does not happen in

seconds, hours, days, or weeks.

Healing takes time.

Happiness takes time.

It takes months, maybe even years—

Especially for broken, lost souls

Like us.

Starving for Sanity

I just need some sanity.

Some soundness of judgement

Something sensible for my soul

Some stability in myself

Something to sway this stress away

I just need

Sanity.

Keilah Belen

Awaiting Destination

If Forever

is a destination,

Then Forever

is where I shall wait.

Cliff Hanger

I know you're tired. I know you've packed everything you thought you'd need to reach the summit of that mountain top.

I know you think you've given everything you've got: physically and mentally. And now you're hanging from a cliff, right? Wondering how and when you could've taken the wrong step.

I know you think this is it, that this is how it ends. And you're looking at the world above you, trying not to look down because you're afraid you might just go along with it.

Sweetie, look up. Look at all that's atop of you and that mountain. The sky. So reach for it. Reach for it. Look deep down inside your core, and find that inner strength. Allow it to take over your whole-being and dent the very edge of that cliff with your fingernails, as you rise above it.

And don't ever be afraid to look back, because this was just another stepping stone on your way to the top. You did it once. You did it twice. You did it multiple times.
You can keep doing it.

So when you reach the peak of that mountain, look down and admire the journey. Then look up and inhale the victory. Keep going, because with the help of God,
you've got Zion to reach.

Keilah Belen

The Soul in Soldier

I'm battling my own war field.
And I can feel the explosions of my own intestines—
Causing an exothermic reaction, releasing all this energy,
Bringing out all this light and heat in me.

All these chemical reactions are sparking me up,
while I'm crawling on my knees, shaking,
trying to find a safe haven.

I made it out alive.
Once again,
That's my spirit.
That's the soldier in me.

<u>Deep Waters</u>

Take a clear look while you're floating
across the surface of this ocean.
Look down,
look way down.

- *Why?*

Just do it.

- *Holy shit.*

All these unknown things
Are the unspoken deep thoughts
That lie within my head—
Scattered and Sunken.

Now you know why I fear the ocean.

Keilah Belen

My Artistry

This blank page

Is my canvas.

This keyboard

Is my paintbrush.

Watch me

Paint pictures

With words.

The Roots and Her Growth

She took her roots,
what was underground her,
and conveyed the nourishment
to her inner soul.

She made her body
her own garden,
and established
a field of everlasting
blossoming flowers.

And in this
She found that her roots
made her who she has
grown to be—

An exquisite
piece of nature.

Keilah Belen

Dig Deeper

Unreachable.

Untouched.

Unmoved.

Her sorrow is buried

Deep underneath her skin.

Take a shovel,

And dig up.

Rise Above the Surface

When roses blossom,
They do not hesitate.

So do not worry too much
About the process.

Because all beautiful things
Eventually grow.

All beautiful things
Rise above the ground.

And all beautiful things
Don't go unnoticed.

Keilah Belen

Home in Your Arms

If you feel safe, secure, and sheltered
In a person's arms,
Never let them go.

Because home is hard
To lay your hands on.

Home is where
The heart is.

And your heart
Is my home.

And it feels
More like home
Than the house
I was raised in.

Exhaling the Toxic

People can be toxic—

whether the toxoid is intentional or unintentional.

That makes no excuse to allow such harmful substance

into your system.

You've already inhaled too much,

And it has dispersed throughout your body.

Think of your heart and health.

Don't be afraid to let go.

Don't be afraid to exhale.

Keilah Belen

Home is Where the Heart Is

Home never leaves.

It is a destination

Where the heart

Feels at peace

When you're lost

Or lonely.

I'm here.

I'm home.

I always will be.

The Broken Will Rise

If you broke someone,

You are not allowed

To tell them how to mend.

They will mend

How they need to be mended,

And they will repair themselves

Stronger than ever

Without you.

Keilah Belen

Her Discoveries in Hurting

She is strong because:

She found companionship in her loneliness;

She found luminosity in her darkness;

She found self-love in her heartbreak;

She found delight in her sadness.

And she will always find a light

At the end of every deep tunnel.

The Night Sky in Me

I find most of myself at night.

This is when all my thoughts connect,

Where all my words unite,

Where my poesy derives from—

Like the stars correlating to make constellations.

And in my head, just like the night sky,

I form many of these.

Keilah Belen

Behind the Empty Hearted

You're lying there,

Curled up in the covers crying.

You're lying there,

Oblivious of why you do so anymore.

Numb.

Vacant.

Hollowed.

Let me tell you something.

It makes sense to feel that way,

When you've given everything

To someone who didn't reciprocate the same,

Leaving you with nothing left.

Love Injection

You said…

I can't reciprocate the same kind of love you give.

But what if I said you do.

Because the moments spent together

Were literally the healing I could use.

And every time I was held by you

Was like a needle to my vein,

Injecting me with love

And curing a little of this pain.

Like all the love I had given out before,

Was being infused and restored with more.

Keilah Belen

A Part of You Everywhere

Missing you is waking up on the other side of the bed because I instantly became accustomed to giving you mine.

Missing you is listening to music with a part of you in it because your love for music is incredible.

Missing you is reading R.h. Sin and R.m. Drake on bus rides with my earphones plugged in.

Missing you is like the beautiful red fiery sunset I saw because that's your favorite color.

Missing you is going to bed, replaying every moment spent together, the words exchanged, and our lips touching.

Missing you is not only missing our kisses, but missing the security felt when held by you—my other half, my best friend—and tearing up because I don't know if I'll ever have that again.

Missing you is going to sleep, leaving a space for you without even realizing it, like I still do in my heart.

Dear Dad

You'll never return.
I hope you feel it burn.
I hope you feel the heat blazing through your veins.
You'll never get it through your fucking brain.

All these fucking years of shedding tears
Shifting emotions, like shifting gears
Mind is always racing, chasing.
Heart is always shaking, aching.

There's a constant replay in my head—
Seriously? A fucking threat? Death?
Scars and bruises remain.
On Mom's brain.
Danny can explain.
He saw you fucking go insane.
The house you couldn't obtain,
But made Mom pay.
Leaving letters on Grandma's windowpane.
Shut your coward ass and don't complain.
You lost your right when you left on that plane.

It's your fault I lost my Faith.
It's your fault I feel this drained.
It's your fault I'm never sane.
Never laid a finger on me, but scars still remain.

I lost you since my childhood days.
I learned that no one ever stays.
You were never here to see me play.
And I think of that every damn day.
Sometimes I feel, Sometimes I don't. Either way I can't display.

Never needed someone to show me affection.
Because with you being absent,
I learned to be independent.
But what's it all for, if I don't feel sufficient.

I'm weak. I'm strong.
Stuck in between feeling right or wrong.
Stuck in feelings where I don't belong.
Filling my ears with lyrics and songs.
I ask myself—How long? How long?

Patience… Patience… Patience…
'til I can't take it and feel like breaking fences.
Maybe I get my raging days from you.
Maybe I'll never make it through.

What type of humankind would leave five behind?
Please realign your fucking mind,
Or at least your sight, because you must be fucking blind.
But you got two other children? Shit. What a fucking mastermind.

I wish I knew from the day Mom gave birth.
I wish I knew since the day I came to this Earth.
I wish I knew you'd strip me of my own worth.
Fuck. I can't. Can't finish this. My heart. It fucking hurts.

Silencing the Heart

When it came to the point

Where I had to decide

To silence my heart

Of my true feelings for you,

I felt the hurt.

All of it.

It's like having something you enjoy the most

Like your favorite beat you created

Or the lyrics to a song you wrote

And having to stop.

That's what silencing my feelings

Feels like.

Do you feel it?

You can't.

All On Me

You are not to blame for this hurt.

I knew the possible outcome.

I was just hoping

For a different turnout.

And that maybe,

Just maybe

You could want me

Like I wanted you.

Hurting for the Hurt

I think the worst kind of pain
Is feeling like you're not enough
Like everything you do isn't right
And everything you say or touch is destroyed

And no matter what you do or say
The people you love cannot be healed
That there is nothing you can do
To help them heal

And if I could
I'd take everyone's pain
Because I've seen it all
And that one more scar
Would be okay
Because everyone I love is hurting
And I can't do anything
This is feeling useless

Keilah Belen

If I Never Get the Chance

Such an irony--
You Feel a lost Feeling.

I notice you've been making friends with death,
But there's so much more than taking your last breath.

All this misery taking control
Of everything inside you as a whole
Making you Feel the emptiness of a hole

Deep inside your chest
You Feel your body truly compress
Through the puffs and sips, you try to decompress

I notice you've been making friends with death,
But there's so much more than taking your last breath.

I got so much hurt.
Words can't ever match.

You might think it's nothing.
But there is something.
For me it's everything.

I notice you've been making friends with death,
But there's so much more than taking your last breath.

Just know that if you ever decide to
I have to be completely honest with you.

Truthfully, you've made an impact in my heart
When life pulled me apart,
You had me from the start.

You shot me like a bull's eye with a dart.

Romantically or not--
You are something that I'll always want.

I notice you've been making friends with death,
But there's so much more than taking your last breath.

If you ever decide to take your life—
Romantically or not--
I love you.

Begging for Mercy

I'm on my knees, I'm praying.
Hoping I can finally see
What this world has come to be
And what is destined to be me.
I'm asking God to bring me mercy,
Anything to set me free.
I'm shouting, I'm yelling, I'm begging.

God, take me back.
God, send me to heaven.

I know I've sinned.
I know I'm cutting my life thin.
I know I'm bleeding inside this skin.
But my soul needs you.
It's asking to go up to the sky so blue.

Notetaking I

Let me tell you something. Whatever you are passionate about initially lies underneath this ground—a seed waiting to develop. If you're truly passionate about someone or something, you will do anything (and I mean anything) to make it work. If you love someone or something, you know that there is nothing realer than having it at the palm of your hands.

You have the power to make it thrive. You hold the water hose to help it grow. It's all on how badly you want it. You can't say you'll always love it, if you don't even invest your time into it. If you don't take care of it, one day it'll be gone. It'll become a memory, something that would do anything just to rise above the surface in search for you. Because you're the only person who holds the watering can, when you drop it and decide you're done, it'll stop growing. It'll be stepped on and won't ever be able to flourish from below the surface. It'll be too late. Just closed off. A seed taken for granted.

So don't ever take what you're passionate about for granted-- any friendship, relationship, etc.-- because it'll slowly start to die right in front of your eyes. The saddest part is that you won't even realize it's dead because your vision was focused far into something else: a distraction that hindered the privilege of watching the most beautiful thing blossom. You've lost the most beautiful thing your eyes have ever met and will meet.

So be consistent. Pay your visits. Water it. Provide the sunlight and water it needs. If you do all these things and support it, you will witness the growth of the most extravagant piece of nature this world has ever been exposed to.

Killer Brain

Where's the strength in me to burgeon

I dissect my own thoughts so detailed like a neurosurgeon

But sometimes I go in too deep

To the point where I'm spewing blood through my eyes

Because I can't hide what lies inside this dark mind

And every day is living proof that I

Am deadly on the inside

But display the opposite on the outside

And I'm sick and tired of scalping my brain

If only people knew that this shit is draining

The life out of me

And I can barely see

Any positivity

Because all that's thrown at me

Is fucking negativity

And I'm

I'm my own enemy

Realization

People don't know

The damage they've done

Until the damage is done.

Lightning Bolt

My presence itself is a lightning rod,
Filled with grace.
I don't have to touch you
To make you see
The miracles coated by my skin.
But when I strike,
Be prepared
Because I will inject you
With extreme heat--
A massive electrical discharge
Too powerful for any human being.
And only the strongest will survive,
Both the exit and the entrance wound:
The ruptures of the blood vessels
And the odd, yet beautiful scarring on the body.
I will make you see
What true love should be--
Withstanding anything this earth can bring.
And that is
Nature in its most daunting purity.

Keilah Belen

Dear Grandma

You clothed me with blouses, skirts and shoes to wear.

You fed me with food
And always had some on the table for everyone.

You showed me strength in the loss of
your husband, siblings, children,
and your battle with cancer.

You always forgive
Others who wrong you,
And you do this so effortlessly.

But in these struggles you have overcome,
You have given me the greatest lessons.

You have clothed me with
Love and humility.

You have fed me
Perseverance and determination.

You instilled diligence
And the importance
Of a forgiving heart.

Thank you for everything
You have been, are, and will continue to be—
A blessing to everyone shot from heaven,
A role model for years to come
For our children, and our children's children.
From the bottom of my heart,
I love you.

A Dying Rose

You spotted me,
With my stem
leaning to the ground
and my petals
slowly falling off.

You poured water
And gave me nutrients,
As I slowly began to blossom.

And when I became stable,
You stopped.

And you moved on
And I…
I became unstable again.

And now
I must wait
To find it
In my roots
And replenish myself
Again.

Keilah Belen

Ghost Poet

I disappear then reappear,
Lingering around,
Wiping my tears,
While I breakdown.

These thoughts keep flowing,
Spinning in circles.
I'm self-loathing,
Jumping hurdle after hurdle.

Same routine.
Repeat, repeat.
No relief, no belief
In Me.

Bring me the extremity
Of pure light or obscurity.
That's all I need
To get the poet out of me.

Viewpoint

These eyes have captured portraits of
satisfaction, and gratification—
weeping tears of joy.

But…

These eyes have captured portraits
Of distress and despair—
Bleeding tears of desperation,

Painting permanent pillow stains.

Lonely Hours

Nobody wants to be alone,
Crying in bed with no one to hold.
Holding back and repeating *don't*.
Convincing yourself you are gold
In the steamiest heat and blistering cold.

Stop crying but you do so,
Because you can't withhold what wants to unfold.

There's no guarantee that you'll feel better tomorrow,
Because there's no control in your sorrow,
So you just hope for a better tomorrow.

Toxic Ozone

Poison in the air

Like the devil says

Take it all. Inhale and share.

That's all this atmosphere subsumes—

Just a bunch of fatal fumes

For us to use and diffuse

Back into this oxygen we misuse

That could be infused for great use.

Keilah Belen

Unfadeable Memories

It's like a tape.

I can't let these memories fade,

But sometimes I wish they did.

Because it's like a stab in the heart with a blade

Every time my mind presses play.

The Battle: Inside vs. Outside III

Body: *Just move on.*

Soul: *How can I?*

How can I move on without my deepest and darkest thoughts?

How can I move on when the person I love dearest holds all of that?

How can I move on with nothing left in me?

Heartbreaks are not simple.

Moving on is not simple.

Love is not simple.

It's not that simple.

Body: *That's the thing sweetheart. It's not simple. It's not supposed to be simple. God will place a battle in your life, one that you must fight with all your strength. You must rely on His love. You must trust in Him. You must keep on loving and caring. You must move on from any hurt your heart holds. And you'll do it because you're a fighter. And you never quit.*

My Potent Poesy

I'm omnipotent to this poetry.
There's power to my pain,
Running through these veins,
Painting pictures in this "perfect" place of mind.
It's this art of mine
That deters my thoughts from getting out of line.

This poesy is a postmortem—
Pasting puzzle pieces of my own perishing mentality.
I'm a student to this speculation of my insanity—
Swiftly searching through these synonyms in my soul.
My words are not just meaningful.
They are powerful.

Tell Me Now

When you come around,

I know you know you turn this frown

Upside down.

So tell me now, tell me now.

Is it me you want to see when you're in town?

Tell me now, tell me now.

Is it me you want to see when you break down?

So come around, come around.

And tell me now, tell me now.

Chin Up

How am I supposed to find the lightness

When all that's inside me is this darkness

How am I supposed to climb these mountains

When these rocks keep tumbling down my spine

Eroding my body like a fucking canyon.

How am I supposed to breathe

When this fucking air is filled with toxicity

Ain't it mind-blowing

How I barely have enough water in me to keep flowing

Yet I keep my head high and keep hoping

That I don't let these demons get the best of me.

Who?

Who catches me when I'm falling?

Who collects my tears when I cry?

Who goes above and beyond to reach the stars for me?

Who matches the love I have to offer?

Giving too much is exhausting.

I'm exhausted.

Keilah Belen

Unfazed Heartbreak

This love doesn't fade.

This pain doesn't go away.

Heartaches play no games

When it comes, it comes with flames.

Nothing can tame the blaze

No not even rain.

It's unfazed.

Euphoric Facade

The route she's taken has gone on
for miles and miles,
stumbling upon stepping stones
while her soul groans
rupturing her ribcage
Bones blown away into this toxic ozone.

It's just masked disheartenment
beneath the vivacity
of her own breathtaking smile.

The Battle: Inside vs. Outside IV

Body: *You're 20. You're young, intelligent, and beautiful. Have fun. Party. Meet boys. You have your whole life ahead of you, so stop worrying too much.*

Soul: *But that's the thing. That's what society wants you to be. That's what this world has created to distract you from the more important things in life. That's not me. I am not for this world. I'm unfit to compete with the bullshit this society wants me to be. I'm me, and I'm not changing. I will have fun how I see fit. I will wait for the Man who makes me a priority not an option. I am beautiful in my own way. Don't tell me how to fix myself. That's for God to take care of.*

Notetaking II

Here's the thing.

You may accept the loss of a relationship,

But some people will never be able to truly move on.

And you just have to accept that not everyone you love will love you the same.

And that not everyone you love is supposed to stay in your life.

It's sad. I know. But that's just how life is.

Keilah Belen

<u>Homeless</u>

Never had a place that felt like home,
But you were home to me.
In your sheltering arms,
I felt unharmed.

But maybe I was never home to you.
And that's something I have to remind myself.
You don't just leave someone you love.
It's like two long-lost souls were separated from the start,
Only to meet again and get ripped away from each other.

Climate Change

You're so cold to me.

How must I find warmth in this silent treatment you are giving me?

For what is this Love you said you felt for me?

Is that how you treat someone who would pray for your heartache to freeze

And disappear into these frozen waters?

Keilah Belen

What We Fear

People aren't afraid to love.

They're afraid to love hard,

And not be loved the same way.

Reminder

Be careful

Who you give

Your heart to.

Keilah Belen

Wish You Were Here

the peaceful ocean breeze

the jungle-like palm trees

the smell of piña coladas

the taste of mojitos

the sand in my feet

The Night in Day

I used to only write at night

But this darkness inside

this furious mind

Has peeked outside

Turning day to night

And now day and night

Is when I write

Keilah Belen

<u>Heartbreak</u>

This heartbreak was the cherry on top
To fall on my knees and drop.
I'm praying. I'm praying to God
To remove me from this pain that's making me rot.
I'm trying. I'm trying not to fall apart.
This ache is too much, I feel it so hard.
When will I start
To yank out these darts
Stuck in my heart.
You said you'd never leave.
Now I'm here contemplating my belief
In love, because if I break again there will be *nothing* left of me.

Moving on from Loss and Heartbreak I

The first step to moving on from loss or heartbreak— whether it's from a friendship or romantic relationship— is accepting the occurrence of the situation. In other words, accepting that the relationship is done. With acceptance comes a lot of pain. This is because you must accept that the person who means dearly to you is no longer the person you may lean on and that this person has been in your life long enough to open up your mind and take what was in it. It is accepting that even though you shared a huge chunk of yourself with that person, they may not even hold that dear to heart as you did. And throughout the process of accepting, I believe that this is the time where you hurt the hardest. And some may say "just accept it and move on", but like I've mentioned before it is not that simple. This is the perfect time to come in grips with your emotions and truly let out all the pain you're feeling— that is crying, being angry, and feeling numb at times from all the tears that have drained your body. Why? Because if you don't allow this to happen, it will catch up to you eventually in the process of moving on, and it will only become more difficult to do so. It is important to remember to take your time while accepting the loss of the relationship, so be patient and let all your tears out. This may take days, weeks, months.

Moving on from Loss and Heartbreak II

The second step to moving on, is doing everything in your power to become distracted of the pain you're feeling. And yes, you may not always be content about the activities or hobbies you're doing, but it's a start. It's a start from not crying day in and day out. It's start from not feeling like you're drowning in your own ocean of tears. You may sometimes even feel numb while trying to fake a smile, because you have no energy left in you to put a grin on your face when all you've done is cry. It sucks. It really does, but within time you will find that somewhere in that smile was a small portion of happiness. Never rush. Do you. Go out. Step out of your comfort zone. Take your time. It's all a process.

Moving on from Loss and Heartbreak III

The third step to moving on, well see that's the thing... I'm still trying to figure it out. I may not even be past step 1 or 2.

But, I'll leave you with this. Be patient with your pain, and be patient with your process in moving on. Not everyone is the same, and not everyone can move on so quickly. Everyone will experience heartbreak or pain at least once in their lifetime in some way, shape, or form. And others are already more broken than others, so please remember to always be kind to yourself and to others, for you do not know which battles they are fighting. Be as patient with them as you are with yourself.

Keilah Belen

Distant

I just want my best friend back.

I can't go through this pain alone,

But this life doesn't always grant us

What we want.

Open Wounds

They ask you to open up,

But fail to stitch up the wounds.

And sometimes this healing

Means being the shoulder to lean on,

The hand to hold, ears to listen,

Or giving a simple response like

"I'm here to hold you".

Keilah Belen

<u>Notetaking III</u>

I must stay true to my colors,

The ones I have painted on my canvas

Growing up.

All my mistakes

And coloring outside the lines

Are what have made me

A beautiful flawed craft.

Phenomenal

I am straight lightning from the clouds,

Striking on this earth.

And trying to keep calm

In my own storm,

Makes me a fucking phenomenon.

Keilah Belen

The Unexpected

I didn't expect to fall so hard

or be ripped apart in pieces this badly.

Even though I knew the risk,

I didn't think it'd be so hard to get back up from.

Because I've been through hell and back,

And I thought a heartbreak wouldn't be this bad.

Now I feel like I'm burning in my own hell

Trying to escape these flames that won't burn out.

__Fighter__

You are strong because you keep fighting,

And you never really know how strong you are

Because that's all you've ever done… is fight.

That's your only option for survival.

Keilah Belen

<u>All Over Again</u>

If you leave, I must now start from square one—

From the acceptance of only being friends

to not having you at all.

And that's even harder.

Your Graveyard

Maybe you couldn't find a home in me

Because you are still grounded

in someone else's backyard

and have not been able to escape

the same way I am grounded in yours

And I cannot dig you out

From underneath that deep hole

Keilah Belen

November

The season changes,

And the leaves fall down

From their branches.

The sun sets,

And the moon rises—

Shorter days

And longer nights.

The day changes,

And the tears fall down

From my face

Like a seasonal change.

I love November,

Because I find November in me

Everyday.

His Showing

Shivering in the covers
She could see nothing but a blur
Of the twinkling lights
Dangling on her wall,
As her eyes poured out waterfalls.
This, of course, was normal.

She laid in bed
Speaking underneath her breath
To the only person who could possibly care.
No answer.
This, of course, was usual.

She placed the book in her hands,
Tucked it into her chest,
With a sharp pain in her heart,
Repeating the verses.
Endless voices in her head
Battling in her brain like a war field.
This, of course, was on the regular.

She closed her eyes,
Still weeping in her own oceans of agony,
Lingering on to the last spark of hope
Deep in her heart.
The night faded away into darkness in her head—
Finally some rest.
This, of course, was familiar.

She flipped over, startled and awoken
By the sound of the flipping pages
That sat beside her as she slept.
Her vision still blurred

Keilah Belen

By the continual tears
And the sudden awakening,
Instinctively focused onto a verse.
This… This was uncommon.
But very alleviating.

The Battle: Inside vs. Outside V

Soul: *How must I pack up all that's left of me and move these legs that have sunken so deep into his soiled souled home?*

Body: *Oh, sweetie. Don't you know by now?*

Soul: *Know what?*

Body: *You have no home. You are unfit for this world. Haven't I told you enough?*

Soul: *But he makes me feel safe and warm. He makes me love, when I haven't loved before. He makes me feel things that I've never felt before. He helps me understand more of myself as he opens his doors and I can resonate. That feels like home to me.*

Body: *Sweetie, no. I know you're tired of packing your bags, moving from house to house all these years, but you have to find it in you and dig yourself out of the hole you have planted in his territory. Home welcomes you, and he has not welcomed you for a while now.*

Soul: *But he promised he wouldn't leave me. Home doesn't leave you.*

Body: *Exactly. And now he pays you back with silence after all you've done, like encourage him, understand the roots that lie beneath his ground, and support him by hammering nails to keep him stable?*

Soul: *You're supposed to do that. You're supposed to help build up your home. It doesn't matter how damaged it is, because with prayer God will help you find warmth in it.*

Body: *I know you don't want to let go, and you're still trying to fix something that is broken, but you've prayed to God already and have asked him to put this at his hands. They say that no message is also a message, and maybe his silence is God's answer to you.*

Soul: *But we should help each other grow; we should help each other find God.*

Body: *That is true sweetie. But you also prayed to help him find himself in whatever way that was, even if it meant letting you go.*

Soul: *So that's it? After everything we've been through... I just drop it?*

Body: *Sweetie, you have done everything you can to help him understand where your hurting is coming from, and if he cannot see that, then yes. You drop it. You allow him to grow on his own.*

Soul: *But what if I never cross his path again, what if I never get to knock on his door and be welcomed again? What if he welcomes someone else in? What if that's never me again?*

Body: *You prayed that if he finds a love, you hope it is a love stronger than yours. The love you have showed is beyond this world. You have prayed for him any way you can. You have prayed he finds his way. You prayed he finds God again. You prayed. The questions you have asked me have already been answered through the words of your prayers. It's just a matter of accepting it. Take your time. Keep praying. Remember you are the queen of patience. You have the key to your own heart and your own home. Focus on rebuilding yourself. What is waiting for you is much better than what any man on this earth could ever offer. The love you have to offer and the love you have given does not go unnoticed. God will welcome you to heaven. Your home.*

Soul: *But I need to tell him one last time. I need to tell him that I love him and that I'm thankful. I'm thankful for the hurting and the healing. I'm thankful for the memories and times spent together.*

Body: *You already have, but if you want to tell him that you love him don't expect him to say it back. There isn't anything you just mentioned that you haven't told him already, and it may hurt. Are you sure you want to put your heart on the line like that?*

Soul: *I've already risked everything. How can I let him know that I love him one last time if he doesn't want to speak or hear from me?*

Body: *This contains a majority of you, your thoughts, your heart, and you've been hesitant about sharing this with him because the distance created has gone too far. You're afraid that if you open up once more, you will hurt more. But listen, you've got this fire burning inside you and you need to let it go. You may not hear from him again, but at least he'll know. You know you've been wanting to, so give him the last piece of you. Give him what you think will always stay with him.*

Soul: *That's the thing. I'm always giving, but when do I receive the same kind of effort?*

Body: *When have you ever asked for anything in return? Sweetheart, you're a giver. You've never been the type to ask for something in return. You give. That's just who you are. And yes, at times you may become distant and not give as much, but you never stop showing the love you have for others, and you do this in ways not many will notice or recognize. You are patient in someone else's anger, and that's because you understand— whether it's a good or bad reason. You understand, and you do this because you wish someone would go out of their way to give you the same. You don't always receive it, and it hurts. But let me tell you something. You shouldn't change who are you because your heart is broken, and although you feel as if you have nothing left in you to give, you keep giving in some way, shape, or form. That's you; it's in your blood. You are meant to give. It warms your heart to know you're giving someone something others can't. You don't even realize you bring light in a dark room. You are full of love, and it's so much to even bare that you want to share it all—every bit of it. I know right now it seems like you have nothing left to give, but here you are writing. Here you are pouring your heart out to some piece of paper. You are genuine, and if someone walks away from you, just remember you are treasure. Don't hesitate to give the last piece of you, and deep inside your heart there is still a beat he created that inspired you to open up the layers of your core. Never change, so just do it. I know it'll take everything in your soul, but once you give him the last piece of you a part of you will let go. Maybe that's why you're so scared. Because if you get no response, then your biggest fear became reality—that the person you loved with all your heart left you after sharing your whole life. It is the most difficult thing to deal with, but you are strong. There isn't anything you haven't overcome. And even if you never get over him, I will be so damn proud of you for giving everything you have and more and still trying even after having your heart ripped out.*

Soul: *Thank you.*

Body: *For what?*

Soul: *For reminding me that I am still alive. For reminding me that I have a purpose in life. For all the encouragement and constant reminders.*

Body: *Do not thank me. I am your shield, remember? And you are my core. Without you I am nothing, I have nothing to contain. I keep you in check, and you keep me in check. Love yourself. Love every bit of you, every flaw. You are beautiful inside and out.*

Made in the USA
Lexington, KY
15 January 2018